"The fear I had was almost like an invitation, a challenge to go forward into something I knew nothing about. . . . In my mind I have always believed that my motion had to be forward."

—MILES DAVIS

MILES DAVIS: JAZZ MASTER

BY PAMELA DELL

Content Adviser: Dr. Chuck Berg, Professor of Theater and Film, University of Kansas, and Jazz Critic

The Child's World

Published in the United States of America by The Child's World®
PO Box 326
Chanhassen, MN 55317-0326
800-599-READ
www.childsworld.com

The Child's World®: Mary Berendes, Publishing Director
Editorial Directions, Inc.: E. Russell Primm, Editorial Director; Emily J. Dolbear,
Line Editor; Katie Marsico, Assistant Editor; Matthew Messbarger, Editorial Assistant;
Susan Hindman, Copy Editor; Sarah E. De Capua, Proofreader; Marsha Bonnoit,
Peter Garnham, Terry Johnson, Chris Simms, and Stephan Carl Wender,
Fact Checkers; Tim Griffin/IndexServ, Indexer; Dawn Friedman,
Photo Researcher; Linda S. Koutris, Photo Selector

The Child's World® and Journey to Freedom® are the sole property
and registered trademarks of The Child's World®

Cover photograph: Miles Davis performing in 1989 / © Derick A. Thomas; Dat's Jazz/Corbis

Interior photographs AP/Wide World Photos: 14, 16, 34; Derick A. Thomas; Dat's Jazz/Corbis: 2;
Underwood & Underwood/Corbis: 12; Marvin Koner/Corbis: 22; Bettmann/Corbis: 28; Nick Elgar/
Corbis: 31; Frank Driggs Collection: 10, 15, 18, 20; Robert W. Kelley/Time Life Pictures/Getty Images: 6;
Hulton|Archive/Getty Images: 8, 19, 21, 25, 27, 32; MPI/Getty Images: 13; Frank Driggs Collection/
Getty Images: 17; AFP/Getty Images: 33, 35; Herb Snitzer/Time Life Pictures/Getty Images: 36;
Courtesy of the Arthur Davenport Black History of Dentistry Collection, Galter Health Sciences Library,
Northwestern University, Chicago, Illinois: 9; Frederick Plaut/MSS 52, The Frederick and
Rose Plaut Papers in the Irving S. Gilmore Music Library of Yale University: 26.

Library of Congress Cataloging-in-Publication Data
Dell, Pamela.
Miles Davis : jazz master / by Pamela Dell.
v. cm. — (Journey to freedom)
Includes bibliographical references (p.) and index.
Contents: Little Davis—Jazz changes—Worldwide fame—Comeback.
ISBN 1-59296-232-7 (library bound : alk. paper) 1. Davis, Miles—Juvenile literature. 2. Jazz musicians—
United States—Biography—Juvenile literature. [1. Davis, Miles. 2. Musicians. 3. African Americans—
Biography. 4. Jazz.] I. Title. II. Series.
ML3930.D33D45 2004
788.9'2165'092—dc22   2003027075

Contents

"Little Davis"

What was it about Miles Davis that earned him the nickname Prince of Darkness? Was it the way he looked? Was it his tendency to lash out at people? Perhaps it was because of his time in the underworld of heroin addiction. Or maybe it was because of the lonely, haunting melodies that he played on his trumpet. It could have been any of these things. Or it could have been all of them together that inspired his nickname. Miles Davis was brilliant, complicated, and shy. He was also a supremely talented musician. Musically, Davis could not sit still. His life was a constantly progressing exploration of sound.

Miles Dewey Davis III was born in the small town of Alton, Illinois, on May 25, 1926. As a baby, he moved with his parents and his older sister, Dorothy, to the town of East St. Louis, Illinois. A few years later, his younger brother, Vernon, was born.

Miles's mother, Cleota Mae Henry Davis, was a music teacher. His father, Miles Dewey Davis Jr., was a successful dental surgeon with three college degrees. Despite the tough economic times of the Great Depression of the 1930s, Dr. Davis's dental practice flourished. The family lived in middle-class comfort, moving later into a white neighborhood. Dr. Davis also purchased a 200-acre (81-hectare) farm outside of town. Miles spent much time there while growing up.

MILES DAVIS, SHOWN HERE PLAYING HIS TRUMPET IN 1958, WAS ONE OF JAZZ'S MOST ORIGINAL AND INFLUENTIAL MUSICIANS. THE WAY HE LIVED HIS LIFE, HOWEVER, WASN'T ALWAYS SO ADMIRABLE.

CELEBRATED VOCALIST BILLIE HOLIDAY SINGS WITH A SMALL JAZZ BAND IN 1939. WHEN MILES DAVIS WAS A TEENAGER, BIG BAND JAZZ WAS THE NEW CRAZE IN POPULAR MUSIC.

As a boy, Miles was interested in many things. He loved fishing, hunting, and riding horses on the family farm. He was a good student who did well in mathematics. His strongest interest was in music. Miles's parents had different ideas about encouraging that interest, however.

Jazz was a new craze sweeping the country then. Like many other people of the day, Cleota Davis believed that jazz was a low-class form of entertainment. She wanted Miles to play violin and to study classical music. Dr. Davis, on the other hand, encouraged his son's interest in music in all forms. He believed that the trumpet would be a good instrument for Miles.

Though Miles's parents argued over what to do, Dr. Davis had the last say in the decision. Before he was 10 years old, Miles was the proud owner of his first trumpet. It was a gift from a family friend.

MILES DEWEY DAVIS JR., HERE IN HIS GRADUATION PHOTOGRAPH FROM DENTAL SCHOOL AT NORTHWESTERN UNIVERSITY IN CHICAGO, ILLINOIS, SUPPORTED HIS SON'S INTEREST IN MUSIC.

IN 1944, MILES DAVIS, SEATED AT THE RIGHT IN THE BACK ROW, WAS HIRED TO PLAY IN EDDIE RANDLE'S ORCHESTRA IN ST. LOUIS, ILLINOIS.

At Crispus Attucks Grade School, Miles began taking weekly trumpet lessons from Elwood Buchanan. A patient of Miles's father, Buchanan had played in bands with some of jazz's hottest musicians. Buchanan had definite ideas about how to play the trumpet. He taught Miles to play clear, round notes, with no **vibrato.** This early influence greatly affected Miles's playing when he was older. He developed a style and a sound that in time became distinctly his own.

Buchanan was a strict and traditional teacher. He encouraged a competitive spirit among his students, and Miles rose to the challenge. Walking to and from school, Miles would often spit peas or grains of rice. This mouth exercise was meant to strengthen his playing. "Little Davis," as he was known around school, was small and shy, but he was driven to be the best horn player of all of them.

By the time he was 15, Miles was playing in the marching band at Lincoln High School in East St. Louis. He carried his horn with him day and night. He practiced constantly and entered every music competition that came along. However, they always seemed to end in disappointment. Each time, the judges chose a white boy as the winner. Like his teacher and others who heard him perform, Miles knew he could—and did— outplay the competition.

Years later, he told a reporter, "It made me so mad I made up my mind to outdo anybody white on my horn. If I hadn't met that **prejudice,** I probably wouldn't have had as much drive in my work. I've thought about that a lot. Prejudice and curiosity have been responsible for what I've done in music."

This motivating force, his curiosity, and his love of jazz fueled Miles's desire to succeed. He soon formed his own small band. By 1940, he was earning money playing in clubs around St. Louis. More than once as a high school student, Miles was invited to tour with bands going on the road. But his parents wouldn't let him leave school, which made the young Miles furious.

By his senior year in high school, Miles had set his hopes on getting to New York, then the heart of the jazz scene. He already had more experience as a musician than most people his age. He had also gained the notice and respect of some major jazz musicians. Two of these young players were alto saxophonist Charlie "Yardbird" Parker and trumpeter John Birks "Dizzy" Gillespie. Miles had first met them at a gig—a paying job playing music—in St. Louis.

Parker, who was six years older than Miles, was especially impressed. He invited the young trumpeter to look him up if he ever came to New York City. This invitation burned in Miles's mind. He knew Parker would help set him up in New York's inner jazz circles. While Miles was thinking about jazz, however, his parents were thinking about college.

Miles's parents had divorced by this time. Again they disagreed on their son's future. Cleota Davis wanted Miles to go to Fisk University like his older sister. Fisk was a well-established university for black students in Nashville, Tennessee. However, Dr. Davis supported his son's wish to attend the famous Juilliard School of Music (then called the Institute of Musical Art). That Miles had chosen Juilliard was not surprising. It was in New York City.

With his father's encouragement, Miles tried out and was accepted at Juilliard. He began classes there in the fall of 1944. Although he was excited to be in New York at last, he found few classes at Juilliard that interested him. The school focused on classical music training. No classes in black music were even offered. Impatient and bored, he began seeking his real music education on New York's 52nd Street.

JAZZ STAR JOHN BIRKS "DIZZY" GILLESPIE POSES WITH HIS TRUMPET IN 1950.

In the 1940s, 52nd Street was known among musicians as **Swing** Street. It was the center of the jazz universe. On any night, the world's best jazz artists played in the many clubs that lined 52nd Street. After arriving in New York, Miles visited these clubs until he successfully tracked down Charlie Parker. Once that happened, Parker took Miles under his wing. Miles Davis had finally found where he belonged.

WHEN MILES DAVIS CAME TO NEW YORK CITY IN THE 1940s, HE FELT AT HOME IN THE JAZZ CLUBS ON 52ND STREET.

Jazz Changes

The more time Miles Davis spent in New York's jazz clubs, the less interested he was in Juilliard. He spent most of his time at school practicing his instrument. In 1945, after the summer semester, Davis dropped out of Juilliard and dove fully into the jazz world.

AFTER HE DROPPED OUT OF MUSIC SCHOOL, MILES DAVIS FOCUSED ON PERFORMING. IN 1949, HE PLAYS AT BIRDLAND. THE FAMOUS NEW YORK CITY JAZZ CLUB WAS NAMED FOR CHARLIE "YARDBIRD" PARKER.

At the time, Dizzy Gillespie and Charlie Parker were leading the way in jazz **innovations.** Swing had been hugely popular in the 1930s and early 1940s. Now jazz's younger players were abandoning this style of jazz for a faster, more unpredictable style of music. Their music came to be known as bebop, or simply **bop.**

DIZZY GILLESPIE WORKS OUT SOME BEBOP MUSIC ON A BLACKBOARD IN **1947.** THIS NEW MUSICAL FORM CALLED BOP GREATLY APPEALED TO MILES DAVIS.

Davis understood and loved this rich, complicated new musical form. One of the most important qualities of bop was **improvisation.** Band members took the spotlight to perform alone, often making up new melodies as they played. Sometimes the other members played softly in the background. These solos—which were rarely the same— brought new sound and energy to each performance.

The loose, improvised style of bop inspired Davis. Bop was a startling breath of fresh air for young listeners. The music was always changing, becoming something new and unexpected.

Compared to bop, swing seemed to Davis—and to many others—stiff and formal. As he played more and more bop, he added his own ideas to the music, changing the style even more.

THE CHANGES IN THE MUSIC INSPIRED MILES DAVIS, WHO PRACTICES IN 1949.

MILES DAVIS BELIEVED THERE WAS GREATER EQUALITY FOR BLACKS IN EUROPE. ANOTHER AMERICAN TRUMPETER, JONAH JONES, PLAYS WITH WHITE MUSICIANS AT THE PARIS JAZZ FESTIVAL IN THE 1940s.

For the next decade, Miles Davis devoted himself to jazz. He played and recorded with one well-established jazzman after another, including Charlie Parker. He formed numerous jazz groups of his own and perfected a **ballad** style that would later make him famous. He toured the United States, spent some time in California, and traveled to France to perform in the Paris Jazz Festival. Davis enjoyed the greater equality between the races that existed there. Though this experience was freeing, it also left him increasingly bitter about racism in the United States.

IN 1949, MILES DAVIS LEADS HIS BAND DURING A RECORDING SESSION FOR *BIRTH OF THE COOL*. THIS ALBUM WAS INFLUENTIAL IN THE DEVELOPMENT OF COOL JAZZ.

In 1949 and 1950, Davis led a series of recordings with a nonet, or nine-piece band. The band's large and unusual horn section gave the music a distinctive sound and style. The pioneering album, called *Birth of the Cool,* produced by Davis and arranged by a white jazzman named Gil Evans, led to yet another musical movement, known as cool jazz.

Cool jazz, or West Coast jazz, was a more mellow sound. It lacked the blaring energy of bop. Although other musicians were also experimenting with cool jazz, Davis gained much of the credit for this new style.

During these years, Davis was enjoying great professional accomplishments. Behind the scenes, however, his personal life was barely staying together. In high school, he had started a relationship with Irene Cawthon that resulted in a daughter, Cheryl, in 1944. Davis left shortly afterward for Juilliard, leaving them behind. In 1946, Irene gave birth to his son, Gregory. She and the children joined Davis in New York in 1947, and in 1950 a second son, Miles IV, was born. But Davis's life was not about family. His whole life centered on jazz—and, increasingly, on hard drugs—and the relationship ended.

ON *BIRTH OF THE COOL,* MILES DAVIS WORKED CLOSELY WITH MUSIC ARRANGER GIL EVANS. THEIR PROFESSIONAL RELATIONSHIP PROVED HIGHLY PRODUCTIVE.

The complicated music Davis wanted to play—so-called modern jazz—was difficult for many listeners to understand. Since the decline of swing, jazz had been losing its audience. Davis refused to play more popular jazz styles. Mostly out of work, frustrated, and bored, he was soon caught in a destructive heroin addiction. One time, desperate for drugs, Davis traded his horn for cash. He stole from trusting friends and sometimes collapsed and lay on city sidewalks, wasted and unable to move.

By 1949, Davis had suffered from his addiction for nearly five years. He sometimes showed up without warning at small clubs and played brilliantly. Then he would reel off into the night, tortured and high. Hoping to kick his habit, Davis retreated to his father's farm in 1953. Recovery lasted only a short time, however, before he gave in to heroin again. But the following year, he had finally had enough.

Davis had always been interested in boxing. To him, famed boxer Sugar Ray Robinson was a hero—a good-looking black prizefighter with plenty of class and self-control. With Robinson as inspiration, Davis took on the battle with drug addiction one last time. "People looked at me with pity and horror," Davis said much later about the years of his addiction. "No one had looked at me like that before."

In 1954, during a brutal 12 days alone in a Detroit, Michigan, hotel room, Davis suffered the vicious pains of withdrawal. At the end of that time, he had kicked his habit. He had beaten heroin for good.

MILES DAVIS STANDS ALONE UNDER A NEW YORK CITY MARQUEE BEARING HIS NAME. DURING HIS LIFE, DAVIS STRUGGLED WITH VARIOUS ADDICTIONS.

Worldwide Fame

In the summer of 1955, Miles Davis walked onstage at the second annual Newport Jazz Festival in Rhode Island. He had been invited to perform at the last minute. Few people outside jazz's inner circle even knew his name. After a heart-wrenching solo on "'Round Midnight," composed by Thelonious Monk, no one in the audience would forget the name Miles Davis. His moving improvisations dazzled the crowd. One music critic wrote that Miles Davis "played thrillingly." Another said "Miles Davis blew beautifully, blew better than anyone else during the three nights" of the festival.

That single historic performance brought Davis widespread public recognition. Within months, Davis had a contract with Columbia Records, a top recording company. For the first time in his life, he had the money he needed to put together a strong five-piece band. His first permanent quintet included Red Garland on piano, "Philly" Joe Jones on drums, Paul Chambers on bass, and John Coltrane on tenor saxophone.

In 1958, Davis made some changes to the lineup of musicians in his band. He also added a second saxophonist, Cannonball Adderley. With this sextet, he issued the landmark album *Kind of Blue* in 1959. On this recording, Davis gave the world the best of modern jazz. More than two million copies of the album sold, a nearly unheard-of feat in jazz.

MILES DAVIS GOT A RECORDING CONTRACT WITH COLUMBIA RECORDS IN 1955. DAVIS HAS A CONTEMPLATIVE MOMENT DURING A RECORDING SESSION IN 1959.

Over the years, the quintets and sextet that Miles Davis put together included several of the finest musicians of the time. Davis produced some of the most important music of his career with these performers. In 1961, at only 35, he had become one of the highest-paid and wealthiest jazz musicians alive.

The 1960s were also a time of personal setbacks. Despite a successful tour in Europe and a heavy concert schedule, Davis went for long periods without recording at all. After the 1963 release of *Quiet Nights,* an album he con-sidered unfinished, Davis refused to record in the studio for almost two years. He had remained free of heroin, but he was abusing alcohol and other drugs and his health was suffering.

In the early 1960s, Davis's parents passed away within two years of each other. A few years later, his wife, dancer Frances Taylor, left him. Though he wed again, in 1968, to 23-year-old Betty Mabry, this marriage lasted only a year. In 1969, he began a four-year relationship with Marguerite Eskridge, with whom he had a third son, Erin.

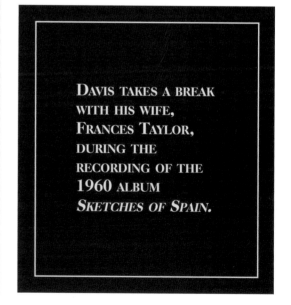

DAVIS TAKES A BREAK WITH HIS WIFE, FRANCES TAYLOR, DURING THE RECORDING OF THE 1960 ALBUM *SKETCHES OF SPAIN.*

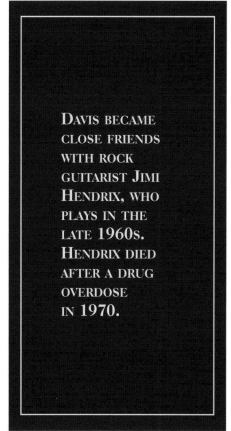

DAVIS BECAME CLOSE FRIENDS WITH ROCK GUITARIST JIMI HENDRIX, WHO PLAYS IN THE LATE 1960s. HENDRIX DIED AFTER A DRUG OVERDOSE IN 1970.

A s the 1960s came to a close, Miles Davis the musician was ready for further changes. Again, he became a pioneer, moving into nearly unexplored territory. Betty Mabry had introduced him to a number of rock and soul musicians including Jimi Hendrix and Sly Stone. Influenced by their music and styles, Davis began adding electric instruments to his music. For the first time, he hired a guitarist to work with him.

With these changes, Davis's music moved away from being strictly jazz. His sound took on a jazz/rock tone. This drastic change upset some jazz fans who believed that Davis had sold out. But he remained at the forefront of change, never looking back. Next, he began experimenting with rhythms based in **funk.**

These experiments grew into the next new jazz style. It was called **fusion** because different musical styles were fused together to create it. Davis's fusion was hugely popular with rock fans. Most had little or no previous interest in jazz. Few of them had ever heard of Miles Davis. All became fans overnight. Innovative young jazz musicians clamored to play with him, while millions of fans packed his concerts.

These developments only added more fuel to the critics' fire. There was no pleasing them. But it didn't matter; Davis was wildly popular. His 1970 album *Bitches Brew* made it to the Top 40 and brought him his first gold record—an honor given only to albums that sell more than 500,000 copies. It also received a Grammy Award, the music industry's biggest honor, for Large-Group Jazz Performance. Davis had won a previous Grammy Award in 1960 for Best Jazz Composition. He went on to receive six more Grammy Awards, and his music topped the jazz recording sales charts several times over.

The success of *Bitches Brew* was the last straw for many of Davis's longtime, older fans. They stopped buying his albums altogether. Some even referred to him as a traitor to jazz. Davis didn't care. "Old people don't buy records," he told a friend during this time. "Young people do."

MILES DAVIS PERFORMS AT A LOS ANGELES NIGHTCLUB IN 1968. AT THIS TIME, THE TRUMPETER WAS EXPERIMENTING WITH FUNK.

The younger music scene energized Davis. By this time, he was often called a living legend, a label he hated. He identified with his young fans and their drive to shake things up. The idea of performing in the same old way, the same old style, year after year was like death to him. Davis's desire and ability to change was a key to his being a great innovator in music.

By the early 1970s, Davis had reached the heights of worldwide fame. At the same time, he had gained a reputation as a difficult, even frightening, man. During performances, he often turned his back to audiences as he played. If anyone approached him hoping to chat, he usually insulted them or swore at them. He never spoke onstage, not even to introduce his band members. It was only in his music that listeners sensed he went deeper. His emotionally charged sound indicated that a sensitive soul was lurking beneath his gruff exterior.

Part of Davis's behavior was a result of his extreme shyness around strangers. Also, in 1956, after an operation to remove small lumps called nodules on his throat, he permanently damaged his voice by shouting at someone. His voice was reduced to a hoarse, raspy whisper that embarrassed him.

But perhaps a deeper reason for Davis's temper lay in the challenge of being black in America. He had grown up in middle-class comfort. He was a major celebrity with talent and intelligence. He had the respect of millions throughout the world. Yet, still he suffered racist insults and humiliations—and even police brutality. In 1959, during a break between sets at a New York City jazz club, Davis was walking a white woman friend to her car when police officers spoke to him in an offensive way. After he responded in his own typical style, they beat him.

Davis was outspoken in his belief that these incidents were racially motivated. Everyone knew that, along with a huge talent, a great anger raged in Davis. They also knew that he had a softer, more open side, although he hid it well. His prickly personality kept people on alert. Fans and friends learned to approach him with caution or leave him alone.

WITH HIS FANS, MILES DAVIS COULD BE DIFFICULT AND ALOOF. HE OFTEN PLAYED CONCERTS WITH HIS BACK TO THE AUDIENCE.

Davis's ongoing physical problems added to his dark side. In 1972, a serious car accident left him with two broken ankles. Other problems followed. By the fall of 1975, Davis had gone through surgery for a second hip replacement as well as another throat operation. Earlier in the year, he had collapsed onstage in Japan from a bleeding ulcer.

Discouraged and depressed, Davis gave up music altogether at the end of 1975. He refused to record or to perform in concert. He didn't play at all. Although Columbia released albums of his previously recorded music, Miles Davis, the brilliant jazz master, had disappeared entirely from the music scene.

A THIN BUT DAPPER MILES DAVIS ARRIVES AT THE AIRPORT IN LONDON, ENGLAND, IN JULY 1973. THE PREVIOUS YEAR, HE HAD BROKEN BOTH ANKLES IN A CAR ACCIDENT.

Comeback

Rumors swirled. Some said Miles Davis was near death. Others waited hopefully for his comeback. Everyone wondered when—or if—the master would return.

It took nearly five years, but Davis did come back. He began with a few unremarkable recording sessions in 1980. It was as if he was stretching muscles that hadn't been used in a long time. Most of that music was never released. But in March 1981, material for a new album was finished. When *The Man with the Horn* was released, Davis began appearing onstage again. The Miles Davis comeback was official.

IN THE EARLY 1980s, DAVIS BEGAN A GRADUAL COMEBACK. HERE HE APPEARS ONSTAGE IN PARIS IN 1982.

For the next several years, he continued to record and perform all over the world. He had cleaned up his drug and alcohol problems—with the support of actress Cicely Tyson, whom he had married in 1981. (They divorced in 1989.) After a stroke temporarily took away the use of his right arm, Davis started painting, and some of his artwork appeared on his album covers. This energetic period captured his fans' attention, but many critics looked negatively on his work.

ACTRESS CICELY TYSON AND MILES DAVIS ATTEND A 1983 MOVIE PREMIERE. THE COUPLE MARRIED IN 1981.

Typically, Davis did not care what others said about him. The only thing he knew how to do was to experiment, change, and question how music was made. Those who couldn't keep up or understand were left behind.

In 1991, Davis began pushing into new territory yet again. He joined with rapper Easy Mo Bee to record a jazz/rap album titled *doo-bop*. It would be Davis's last studio recording.

In the summer of 1991, Davis made another noteworthy shift. For the first time, he stopped looking forward and began looking back. At the jazz festival in Montreux, Switzerland, in July, he performed music he had created more than 30 years earlier with Gil Evans, who had turned out to be one of his greatest collaborators. Two days later, he did a **retrospective** concert in Paris. During this concert, many great musicians who had played in his bands in the 1960s joined Davis onstage. In August, he performed at the Hollywood Bowl in Los Angeles.

IN JULY 1991, MILES DAVIS PLAYS A MUTED TRUMPET IN A PARIS CONCERT.

These concerts puzzled many people. Why was jazz's most determined **visionary** suddenly looking into his past? Some believed they had the answer the following month.

In early September, Davis entered the hospital with bronchial pneumonia. After suffering a massive stroke there, he went into a coma. He never came out of the coma. Davis died at St. John's Hospital and Health Care Center in Santa Monica, California, on September 28, 1991. He was 65 years old. Some of his friends believed that Davis had sensed death coming, which might have caused him to revisit his earlier work.

Miles Davis's impact on the world—at least on the world of jazz—was vast. For 40 years, he was a major force behind many of the important changes in the music. His influence was so great that some believed that, after his death, jazz had lost its direction. They said that without Miles Davis around to push the music, it had lost its energy and tended to sound the same. To his millions of fans, the world of music is darker now, without the Prince of Darkness there to give it light and heat.

Timeline

1926	Miles Dewey Davis III is born on May 25, in Alton, Illinois.
1944	Davis leaves East St. Louis, Illinois, to attend the Juilliard School of Music (then the Institute of Musical Art) in New York City. He spends most of his time in jazz clubs on 52nd Street.
1945	Davis drops out of Juilliard to focus on jazz.
1947	Davis leads a band for the first time, with Charlie Parker on alto saxophone.
1949–1950	Davis leads a series of recordings that become the pioneering album *Birth of the Cool.*
1953	Davis makes his first recording of "'Round Midnight."
1954	After 12 days alone in a Detroit, Michigan, hotel room, Davis kicks his heroin addiction.
1955	Davis gives a historic performance at Rhode Island's Newport Jazz Festival. He forms his first permanent quintet and signs with Columbia Records.
1956	After a throat operation, Davis permanently damages his voice by shouting at someone.
1958	Davis forms a highly respected sextet.
1959	Davis issues the landmark album *Kind of Blue.*
1961	At 35, Davis becomes one of the highest-paid and wealthiest jazz musicians alive.
1963	Davis makes frequent changes to his band lineup. Angered over the release of *Quiet Nights,* an album he considers unfinished, Davis refuses to record in the studio for almost two years.
1967	Davis begins experimenting with longer musical forms and adds a guitarist to his mix.
1968	Davis records *Miles in the Sky* with keyboardist Herbie Hancock.
1970	Davis releases the best-selling *Bitches Brew,* which becomes a gold record in 1976.
1972	Davis breaks both ankles in a car accident.
1975	Davis collapses onstage in Japan from a bleeding ulcer. After surgeries on his throat and hip, Davis does not perform or record for five years.
1981	Davis returns to the public eye with concert appearances and studio recordings. He marries actress Cicely Tyson.
1982	After a stroke temporarily takes away the use of his right arm, Davis starts painting.
1986	Davis wins a Grammy Award for Best Jazz Instrumental Performance for *Tutu.* He appears on the television drama *Miami Vice* and in award-winning Honda commercials.
1988	Davis keeps up a heavy concert schedule. His paintings are exhibited at shows in Japan, Spain, and Germany.
1989	*Miles: The Autobiography* is published and wins the American Book Award. Davis and Tyson divorce.
1991	Davis starts working with rapper Easy Mo Bee on a jazz/rap recording, which is released in the fall (after his death). At summer concerts, he performs material from 30 years earlier in his career. On September 28, Miles Davis dies at a hospital in Santa Monica, California, after suffering from pneumonia and a massive stroke.

Glossary

ballad (BAL-uhd)
A ballad is a popular song with romantic themes. Miles Davis was famous for his ballad style.

bop (BOP)
Bop, short for bebop, is a style of jazz with unusual rhythms, a quick pace, and much improvisation. Jazzmen Dizzy Gillespie and Charlie Parker led the development of bop in the early 1940s.

funk (FUNK)
Funk is music with roots in traditional black music, such as gospel, blues, and soul. At the end of the 1960s, Miles Davis experimented with rhythms based in funk.

fusion (FYOO-zhuhn)
Fusion is popular music that blends different styles, such as rock with jazz. Davis's fusion was hugely popular with rock fans.

improvisation (im-prov-uh-ZAY-shuhn)
Improvisation is the ability to compose or create new music on the spot, often using the basic chords of a specific song as a guide. One of the most important qualities of bop is improvisation.

innovations (in-uh-VAY-shuhnz)
Innovations are new ideas or inventions. When Miles Davis moved to New York City in 1944, alto saxophonist Charlie Parker and trumpeter Dizzy Gillespie were leading the way in jazz innovations.

jazz (JAZ)
Jazz is an American music that developed from ragtime and blues music in the early 1900s. It features syncopated or irregular beats and accents, improvisation, and an instrumental style that often imitated the voice. From an early age, Miles Davis was interested in jazz.

prejudice (PREJ-uh-diss)
Prejudice is a fixed or unfair opinion about someone based on race or religion. Miles Davis said that prejudice and curiosity were responsible for his contributions in music.

retrospective (RE-troh-SPEK-tiv)
A retrospective is a kind of performance or show of an artist's work done over many years. In 1991, Miles Davis did a retrospective concert in Paris.

swing (SWING)
Swing is a style of jazz first played by big dance bands in the late 1920s to the early 1940s. In the 1940s, 52nd Street, the center of the jazz universe, was known as Swing Street.

vibrato (vih-BRA-to)
Vibrato is a pulsating effect in a voice or an instrument. As a boy, Miles Davis learned to play clear, round notes on his trumpet, with no vibrato.

visionary (VIZH-uhn-ar-ee)
A visionary is someone who is able to think ahead to see new possibilities or ideas. Miles Davis is often called a jazz visionary.

Index

Further Information

Books

Asirvatham, Sandy. *History of Jazz.* Bromall, Penn.: Chelsea House Publishing, 2003.

Frankl, Ron. *Miles Davis.* Bromall, Penn.: Chelsea House Publishing, 1995.

Gourse, Leslie. *Blowing on the Changes: The Art of the Jazz Horn Players.* Danbury, Conn.: Franklin Watts, 1997.

Weatherford, Carole Boston. *The Sound That Jazz Makes.* New York: Walker & Company, 2000.

Web Sites

Visit our homepage for lots of links about Miles Davis:

http://www.childsworld.com/links.html

Note to Parents, Teachers, and Librarians:
We routinely verify our Web links to make sure they're safe,
active sites—so encourage your readers to check them out!

About the Author

Pamela Dell has published 22 books for children, both fiction and nonfiction, and has also created award-winning educational and entertainment software for children. She divides her time between Santa Monica, California, and Chicago, Illinois.